The Tale of the Turnip

Retold by Jenny Giles

Illustrated by Chantal Stewart

NELSON PRICE MILBURN

Once upon a time,
an old man
planted some turnip seeds.

The sun shone,
and the rain fell,
and soon the seeds
began to grow.

But one of the turnips grew bigger than the others.

It grew and it grew until it was enormous.

5

One day,
the old man said,
"Let us have some turnip soup."

And he went out into the garden to pull up the enormous turnip.

He pulled...
and he pulled...
but the enormous turnip
would not come up
out of the ground.

So the old man asked his wife
to come and help him.

The old woman
held on to the old man,
and the old man
held on to the turnip.

They pulled and they pulled,
And they both gave a shout,
But they still couldn't make
The big turnip come out.

So the old woman
asked the little boy
to come and help.

The little boy
held on to the old woman,
and the old woman
held on to the old man,
and the old man
held on to the turnip.

They pulled and they pulled,
And they all gave a shout,
But they **still** couldn't make
The big turnip come out.

So the little boy
asked the little girl
to come and help.

The little girl
held on to the little boy,
and the little boy
held on to the old woman,
and the old woman
held on to the old man,
and the old man
held on to the turnip.

*They pulled and they pulled,
And they all gave a shout,
But they **still** couldn't make
The big turnip come out.*

So the little girl
asked the cat
to come and help.

The cat
held on to the little girl,
and the little girl
held on to the little boy,
and the little boy
held on to the old woman,
and the old woman
held on to the old man,
and the old man
held on to the turnip.

They pulled and they pulled,
And they all gave a shout,
But they **still** couldn't make
The big turnip come out.

So the cat asked a little mouse
to come and help.

The mouse held on to the cat,
and the cat
held on to the little girl,
and the little girl
held on to the little boy,

and the little boy
held on to the old woman,
and the old woman
held on to the old man,
and the old man
held on to the turnip…

They pulled and they pulled,
And they all gave a shout,

And, **this** time...
  yes, **this** time,
    the turnip came out.

And that night,
the old man,
and the old woman,
and the little boy,
and the little girl,
and the cat,
and the mouse...

...all had turnip soup
for dinner.

A play
The Tale of the Turnip

People in the play

Reader

Old Man

Old Woman

Little Boy

Little Girl

Cat

Mouse

Reader

Once upon a time,
an old man
planted some turnip seeds.
The sun shone,
and the rain fell,
and soon the seeds
began to grow.
But one turnip
grew bigger than all the others.
It grew and grew
until it was enormous.

Old man

Let's have some turnip soup.
I'll go out into the garden
and pull up
the enormous turnip.

Reader

The old man pulled...
and pulled...
but the enormous turnip
would not come up
out of the ground.
So he called to his wife
to come and help him.

Old man

Wife! Wife!
Please come and help me
pull up the enormous turnip.

Old woman

I will hold on to you.

Old man

And I will hold on to the turnip.

Reader

They pulled and they pulled,
And they both gave a shout,
But they still couldn't make
The big turnip come out.

So the old woman
called to the little boy.

Old woman

Little boy! Little boy!
Please come and help us
pull up the enormous turnip.

Little boy

I will hold on to you.

Old woman

I will hold on to the old man.

Old man

And I will hold on to the turnip.

Reader

They pulled and they pulled,
And they all gave a sh<u>ou</u>t,
But they **still** couldn't make
The big turnip come out.

So the little boy
called to the little girl.

Little boy

Little girl! Little girl!
Please come and help us
pull up the enormous turnip.

Little girl

I will hold on to you.

Little boy
I will hold on to the old woman.

Old woman
I will hold on to the old man.

Old man
And I will hold on to the turnip.

Reader
They pulled and they pulled,
And they all gave a shout,
But they **still** couldn't make
The big turnip come out.

So the little girl
called to the cat.

Little girl
Cat! Cat!
Please come and help us
pull up the enormous turnip.

Cat
I will hold on to you.

Little girl
I will hold on to the little boy.

Little boy
I will hold on to the old woman.

Old woman

I will hold on to the old man.

Old man

And I will hold on to the turnip.

Reader

They pulled and they pulled,
And they all gave a shout,
But they **still** couldn't make
The big turnip come out.

So the cat called to the mouse.

Cat

Mouse! Mouse!
Please come and help us
pull up the enormous turnip!

Mouse

I will hold on to you.

Cat

I will hold on to the little girl.

Little girl

I will hold on to the little boy.

Little boy

I will hold on to the old woman.

Old woman

I will hold on to the old man.

Old man

And I will hold on to the turnip.

Reader

They pulled and they pulled,
And they all gave a shout,
And, **this** time…
yes, **this** time…
the turnip came out!

All

Hooray! Hooray!
At last the turnip is out!

Reader

And that night,
the old man,
and the old woman,
and the little boy,
and the little girl,
and the cat,
and the mouse...
all had turnip soup
for dinner.